THE LIGHT THAT SHINES FOREVER

THE TRUE STORY AND REMARKABLE RESCUE OF
669 CHILDREN ON THE EVE OF WORLD WAR II

OTHER BOOKS IN THE TABERNACLE CHOIR CHRISTMAS SERIES

Silent Night, Holy Night: The Story of the Christmas Truce • As narrated by Walter Cronkite

A Christmas Bell for Anya • As narrated by Claire Bloom

I Heard the Bells on Christmas Day • As narrated by Edward K. Herrmann

In the Dark Streets Shineth: A 1941 Christmas Eve Story • Written and narrated by David McCullough

Good King Wenceslas • As read by Jane Seymour

Christmas from Heaven: The True Story of the Berlin Candy Bomber • As read by Tom Brokaw

God Bless Us, Every One! The Story behind "A Christmas Carol" • As read by John Rhys-Davies

The Little Match Girl • As narrated by Rolando Villazón

It Is Well with My Soul • As narrated by Hugh Bonneville

Keepsake Christmas Stories: Holiday Favorites as Performed with The Tabernacle Choir • Featuring 13 Guest Narrators

Come to Him This Holy Night: Three Irish Christmas Traditions • As performed by Neal McDonough

 The Tabernacle Choir at Temple Square provides artistic expressions of faith from
The Church of Jesus Christ of Latter-day Saints.

Library of Congress Cataloging-in-Publication Data

Names: Warner, David T. (David Terry), 1963– author.

Title: The light that shines forever: the true story and remarkable rescue of 669 children on the eve of World War II / David T. Warner.

Description: Salt Lake City, Utah: Shadow Mountain, [2023] | Summary: "A recounting of the story of Sir Nicholas Winton, an English stockbroker who arranged for the transport of nearly 700 children who would otherwise have been sent by the Nazis to concentration camps in the late 1930s. From the 2022 The Tabernacle Choir at Temple Square Christmas concert"— Provided by publisher.

Identifiers: LCCN 2023015438 | ISBN 9781639931392 (hardback)

Subjects: LCSH: Winton, Nicholas, 1909–2015—Juvenile literature. | World War, 1939–1945—Jews—Rescue—Juvenile literature. | World War, 1939–1945—Children—Juvenile literature. | Jewish children in the Holocaust—Juvenile literature. | BISAC: JUVENILE NONFICTION / History / Holocaust | JUVENILE NONFICTION / Biography & Autobiography / Social Activists

Classification: LCC D804.66. W56 W37 2023 | DDC 940.53/18092 [B]—dc23/eng/20230505

LC record available at https://lccn.loc.gov/2023015438

Printed in China
RR Donnelley, Dongguan, China   6/2023

10 9 8 7 6 5 4 3 2 1

THE LIGHT THAT SHINES FOREVER

THE TRUE STORY AND REMARKABLE RESCUE OF
669 CHILDREN ON THE EVE OF WORLD WAR II

WITH FOREWORD BY

SIR DAVID SUCHET

AND AFTERWORD BY

NICK WINTON JR.

AS PERFORMED BY

THE TABERNACLE CHOIR AT TEMPLE SQUARE

WRITTEN AND ILLUSTRATED BY

DAVID T. WARNER

SHADOW
MOUNTAIN
PUBLISHING

FOREWORD BY SIR DAVID SUCHET

I was privileged to tell this true story as part of an annual concert of The Tabernacle Choir at Temple Square. Along with those who attended the live presentation, I'm grateful it will continue to be shared on television and streaming services for many years to come. Even though it is about events that took place just before World War II, the theme and circumstances of the story are not unfamiliar. It is an account of refugee families, driven from their homes in search of safety for themselves and a future for their children. Indeed, it is a story for our time.

So often, religious beliefs, cultural backgrounds, historical traditions, and so forth, are excuses to divide ourselves from one another. But, like light itself, God's love shines on all people, everywhere. And when we share that light by serving others—including with those who are different from us—the light of goodness has an infinite reach and influence.

In the concert, as I finished telling this story, I invited everyone who wanted to share light through service to turn on the lights of their phones. "Hold them up high," I said. It was a profoundly moving sight. Of course, it was impressive to see 15,000 people all doing the same thing at the same time. But what inspired me most was that by holding up our lights together, as one, the darkness disappeared. We were *all* bathed in light.

Which is to say, wherever we come from, whatever our faith, as we work together to serve each other, the darkness of prejudice, hate, and fear will disappear. And that makes this a story about more than several hundred people doing good eighty years ago. It's also a story about each of us here and now, if we want it to be.

David

SIR DAVID SUCHET

In the final months of 1938, the shadow of war was spreading across Europe. Hitler's armies had marched into the borderlands of Czechoslovakia, forcing Jewish families, among others, to flee their homes and seek refuge inland. That winter, as the light of Hanukkah and Christmas drew near, so did the darkness of ethnic cleansing.

Meanwhile, 800 miles away in London, a twenty-nine-year-old English stockbroker, Nicholas Winton, was preparing for a ski vacation in Switzerland.

But just days before his departure, a friend called from Prague. "Nicky," he said, "forget the skis. You need to see what's happening here."

Nicky, the son of Jewish-German immigrants, had a background in international banking and was fluent in German and French. Long interested in world politics, he was naturally curious and immediately changed his plans.

Nicky arrived in the Czech capital on New Year's Eve. There, in the throes of winter, he found sprawling encampments of refugee families—mostly Jewish—huddled in tents and makeshift huts.

At best, they were trapped. Visas for adults were nearly impossible to obtain, much less for entire families. Some wanted to escape, and others were determined to stay, but most agreed something had to be done to safeguard their children now, before it was too late.

Nicky turned this problem over in his mind: "If it's not impossible," he thought, "then there must be a way to do it."

Working with other organizations, a plan emerged: By special waiver, children could leave the country without their parents, as long as host families abroad took them in.

As word of the plan spread, parents lined the hallways and staircases of Nicky's hotel, begging for their little ones to be included. If they could get their children out of the country safely, they would find a way to join them.

Three weeks later, when Nicky's holiday vacation came to an end, he carried home the names and photographs of literally hundreds of children, entrusted to him by their parents.

B ack in London, Nicky worked at the stock exchange by day and coordinated the rescue by night. To expedite the effort, he borrowed stationery from the British refugee committee, adding the words "Children's Section" and calling a meeting of one to appoint himself "Honorary Secretary."

Using that title, he wrote to various governments for help. Several declined, but the British Home Office agreed—as long as Nicky provided a £50 guarantee for each child—the equivalent of more than four thousand American dollars today.

With the assistance of his mother and a growing circle of helpers, Nicky threw himself into recruiting host families, raising funds, and securing visas. For nine months the work continued. And for nine months, children traveled by train and ferry to England.

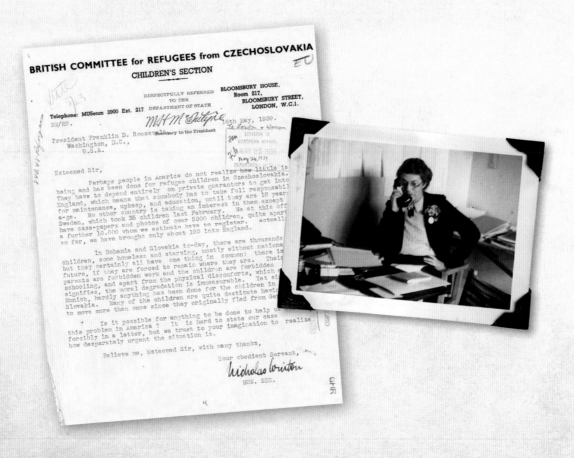

Among the most moving images of Nicky's service are parents on the train platforms at Prague's Wilson Station. Hiding their grief, they took their children in their arms, assured them of an exciting adventure ahead, and promised to be reunited soon.

Through that spring and summer of 1939, as train whistles blew and steam filled the skies, parents waved goodbye, pleading for the strength that only God could provide.

All too soon, war was declared, and the Czech border closed. At final count, 669 children had been rescued. With few exceptions, their families perished, never to be seen again.

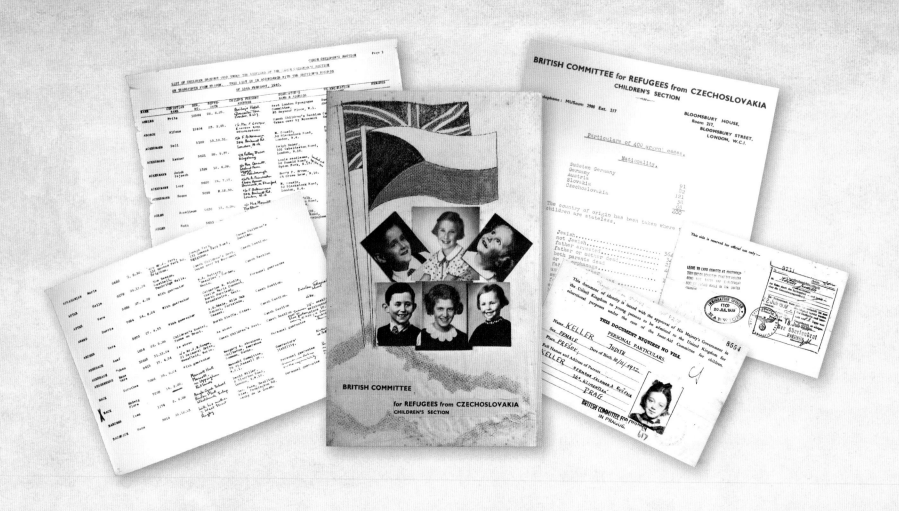

The only record of the rescue was a scrapbook made by one of Nicky's team members. The book's pages were brimming with lists of children, emigration passes, diplomatic correspondence, and so on.

But Nicky was not focused on the past. He was thinking about the future. So the scrapbook went into the attic, and Nicky moved on with his life.

He married, had three children, worked in local business and government affairs, organized assistance for the disabled and elderly, and went about doing good wherever a need was found.

F or some fifty years Nicky rarely spoke of his rescue work, and when he did, it was only in passing.

In the months before Nicky's eightieth birthday, his wife, Grete, found herself in the attic sorting papers. There, in a worn leather case, she discovered the scrapbook. Needless to say, she was astonished. *Who were these children*, she wondered, *and why don't I know about them?*

"It happened so long ago," Nicky explained. "Quite frankly, I haven't given the episode much thought since."

As they talked, they agreed that the book—and the history in it— had to be preserved. With the help of a well-known Holocaust expert, the story began to come to light. Eventually, the BBC invited Nicky to appear on a television program called *That's Life*. And what happened next was a surprise, even to Nicky himself.

During the program, the host told Nicky's story and introduced a few of the rescued children—now in their fifties and sixties. Nicky had never met them, and they had not met him. As they embraced one another, they wept.

Then the host turned to everyone else in the studio. "Is there anyone in our audience who owes their life to Nicholas Winton? If so, could you stand up, please?"

Most of the audience rose to their feet. As Nicky turned to see them, it became clear that he had done more than rescue nameless, faceless children. He had saved a generation of people who had gone on to live productive, meaningful lives—people who now had families and children of their own.

In his final years, Nicky was continually surrounded by these and many more honorary children and grandchildren, all grateful to finally understand the story of their lives.

Though Nicky was knighted by Queen Elizabeth and often referred to as the "British Schindler," he rejected adulation. "I am not a hero," he insisted. "I just did what needed to be done."

When Nicky died at the age of a hundred and six, most of the original children had still not been found. But the known posterity of his rescued family numbered over six thousand.

In time, Nicky's scrapbook was placed in Yad Vashem, the World Holocaust Remembrance Center in Jerusalem. In that setting, his wartime service shines as it should, in memory of the parents and families who sacrificed to save their children.

Nicky was once asked, "Why did you keep the scrapbook a secret?"

"I didn't keep it a secret," he said. "I just didn't talk about it." Perhaps that's because Nicky knew he had more good to do in his life, more than could be contained in any book—for gifts of goodness are truly endless. As we are blessed, we bless others. And the giving goes on.

During that last winter before the war, Jewish parents in Czechoslovakia were not able to celebrate Hanukkah in all the customary ways. But they knew that in the Hanukkah menorah, the single center candle lights all of the others. The light of God's goodness in just one person can bring light to many, now and for generations to come.

Which invites us to ask these questions of ourselves: What light will we bring to others? What stories will fill the scrapbooks of our lives? For some, it will be helping refugees in war-torn lands. For others, it will be visiting a lonely neighbor or lifting up a downcast friend. Whatever we do, the spark of our tiny effort can fill this world with light and write a story of hope and peace that never ends.

This year, as you dedicate yourself to sharing God's light through service to others, consider making a scrapbook of your own. Remember the people who have served you, and those you have been blessed to serve.

You can gather photos from your device into a digital album or store them on a dedicated portable drive. Or make a physical or digital scrapbook to inspire the ones you love. Let those who come after you discover how our stories of service go on—and the light we share shines forever.

ACTIVE GOODNESS BY NICK WINTON JR.

Nick Winton Jr., eldest son and last living child of Sir Nicholas Winton.

Stories of remarkable accomplishments, like those of my father, offer captivating glimpses into slices of history. As time passes, the impact of his particular experience has only grown more significant.

As his son, I believe that the enduring inspiration of his service stems from its fundamental simplicity. At its core, it is a narrative of an ordinary man rescuing the victims of "bad people" engaged in "bad deeds"—a quintessential "hero's journey."

Yet my father never considered his actions to be in the least heroic. He maintained that anyone would have done the same under those circumstances. While the challenge was immense, his belief was that "if something isn't fundamentally impossible, then there must be a way of doing it."

The key distinction between him and many of us lies in his response to adversity. While others might lament the terrible plight of those destitute souls shivering beneath canvas tents in the biting winter cold with scarce food and bleaker prospects, he resolved to take matters into his own hands, as no one else seemed to be stepping up.

Nicholas Winton, while while working with the Red Cross, having assisted in the Dunkirk evacuation.

In one of his letters from that pre-war time he wrote, "There is a difference between passive goodness and active goodness which is, in my opinion, the giving of one's time and energy in the alleviation of pain and suffering. It entails going out, finding and helping those in suffering and danger and not merely leading an exemplary life, in the purely passive way of doing no wrong."

To my father, being a good person necessitated actively helping others instead of merely refraining from wrongdoing.

In our world today, countless people are in need, and the state-provided safety net in some countries often prompts our contemporaries to declare, "Someone should do something about that!" A better response when we encounter someone in need would be for us to adopt the mantra: "What can I do that would make a difference?"

Rescued children arriving by ferry in Harwich, 1939.

Sometimes, all that is required is a kind word of encouragement; other times, more help may be needed.

There exists a rich tradition of philanthropy, which often entails offering financial aid to those in need. However, the gift of our time is frequently more valuable. My father's work is a reminder that each of us possesses the power to change the world—perhaps in small ways, but to the recipient of our kindness it may mean the difference between a world brimming with vibrant colours and one shrouded in the gloom of gray and black.

Embracing the lessons of his story, let us all be more proactive in our pursuit of goodness and extend our hands in support to those in need. The world may seem bleak at times, but with our collective efforts, we can bring light and warmth to even the darkest corners.

NICK WINTON JR.

www.nwinton.com

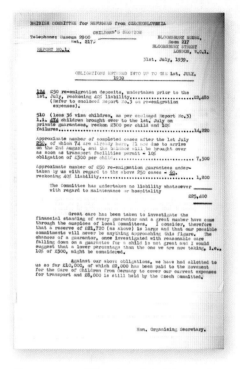

Summary of funds raised through guarantors, July 1939.

CHRISTMAS WITH THE TABERNACLE CHOIR

For over twenty years, Christmas lovers around the world have looked forward to the latest broadcast of *Christmas with the Tabernacle Choir*—the annual holiday concert of The Tabernacle Choir and Orchestra at Temple Square. Each December in the Conference Center of The Church of Jesus Christ of Latter-day Saints, these concerts thrill live audiences of over 60,000. But across the world, millions watch them on PBS through the Choir's partnership with GBH and BYU Television and through select excerpts on Choir's popular social channels.

As host, the internationally renowned Choir and Orchestra are pleased to feature solo artists from stage, screen, and television. These include Broadway singers and actors Alfie Boe, Kristin Chenoweth, Santino Fontana, Sutton Foster, Megan Hilty, Angela Lansbury, Brian Stokes Mitchell, Kelli O'Hara, Laura Osnes, and Lea Salonga; opera stars Renée Fleming, Nathan Gunn, Frederica von Stade, Bryn Terfel, Rolando Villazón, and Deborah Voight; Grammy Award–winner Natalie Cole, *American Idol* finalist David Archuleta; and The Muppets® from *Sesame Street*®. The concerts have also welcomed acclaimed actors Claire Bloom, Hugh Bonneville, Peter Graves, Edward Herrmann, Martin Jarvis, Neal McDonough, John Rhys-Davies, Jane Seymour, Sir David Suchet, Richard Thomas, and Michael York; famed broadcast journalist Tom Brokaw, Pulitzer Prize–winning author David McCullough, and noted TV news anchorman Walter Cronkite.

At the heart of the celebration are 360 Choir members and a roster of more than 200 Orchestra members. These unpaid volunteers are men and women from many countries, backgrounds, and professions who perform over 50 times each year in live concerts, broadcasts, recordings, and world tours. In major performances they are often joined by The Bells at Temple Square, a 32-member handbell choir. Together, these musicians are dedicated to the mission of sharing inspired music throughout the world—music that has the power to heal, comfort, strengthen, and bring people closer to the divine.

Among its many performances, The Tabernacle Choir's weekly *Music & the Spoken Word* program is the longest-running continuous broadcast in history, and includes Spanish and Portuguese versions with voice-over translation in other languages. Five of the Choir's recordings have achieved "gold record" and two have achieved "platinum record" status. Its recordings have reached the #1 position on *Billboard*® Magazine's classical lists a remarkable fifteen times since 2003. Today, music from the Choir and Orchestra is available through the Choir's YouTube channel, Spotify, Apple Music, Amazon Music, and Pandora.

To watch the broadcast performance of the story in this book featuring Sir David Suchet, the Choir, Orchestra, and special guest Nick Winton Jr., please visit TabChoir.org/LightShinesForever.

SIR DAVID SUCHET

David Suchet, eminent stage, screen, and television actor, is best known for his role as the engaging, suave, and precise Hercule Poirot in more than 70 episodes of *Agatha Christie's Poirot* over 24 years. Suchet has received many awards and nominations for his decades of work on stage. He has played characters such as Iago in *Othello*, Shylock in *The Merchant of Venice*, Caliban in *The Tempest*, Bolingbroke in *Richard II*, and Angelo in *Measure for Measure*. All were nominated for Olivier Best Actor Awards. In 2011, Queen Elizabeth awarded him Commander of the Order of the British Empire and in 2020 Knight Bachelor of the Order of the British Empire for his services to drama and charity.